For my loving daughters Sehej and Rehet

This copy belongs to

First Edition 2024

Paperback ISBN: 978-1-0687653-0-8

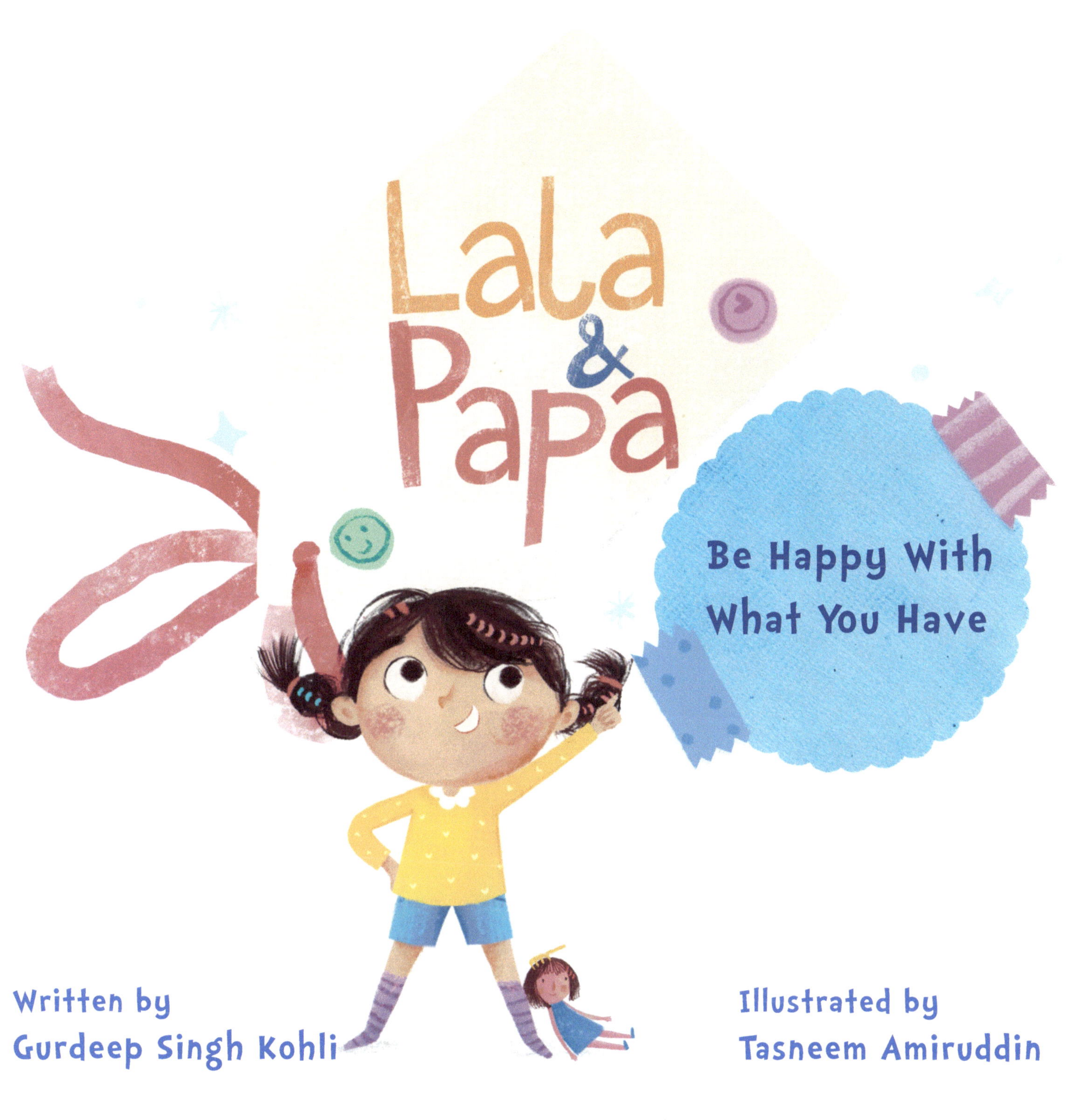
Lala
&
Papa
Be Happy With
What You Have
Written by
Gurdeep Singh Kohli
Illustrated by
Tasneem Amiruddin

Lala's
ROOM

Papa went to Lala’s room
'Get ready! we need to go

It's Nina's birthday tomorrow
And we don't have a present you know!’

‘So first we should go shopping

To buy her something nice

Since she is your best friend

Let's pick something of your choice?'

'Hurray'! shouted Lala

‘I know exactly what we should buy

Can we also get something for me
How about that dinosaur toy?'

'I know you love that dinosaur', said Papa

'But we can't buy that today

You just got gifts on your birthday
I'm sure you have enough to play!'

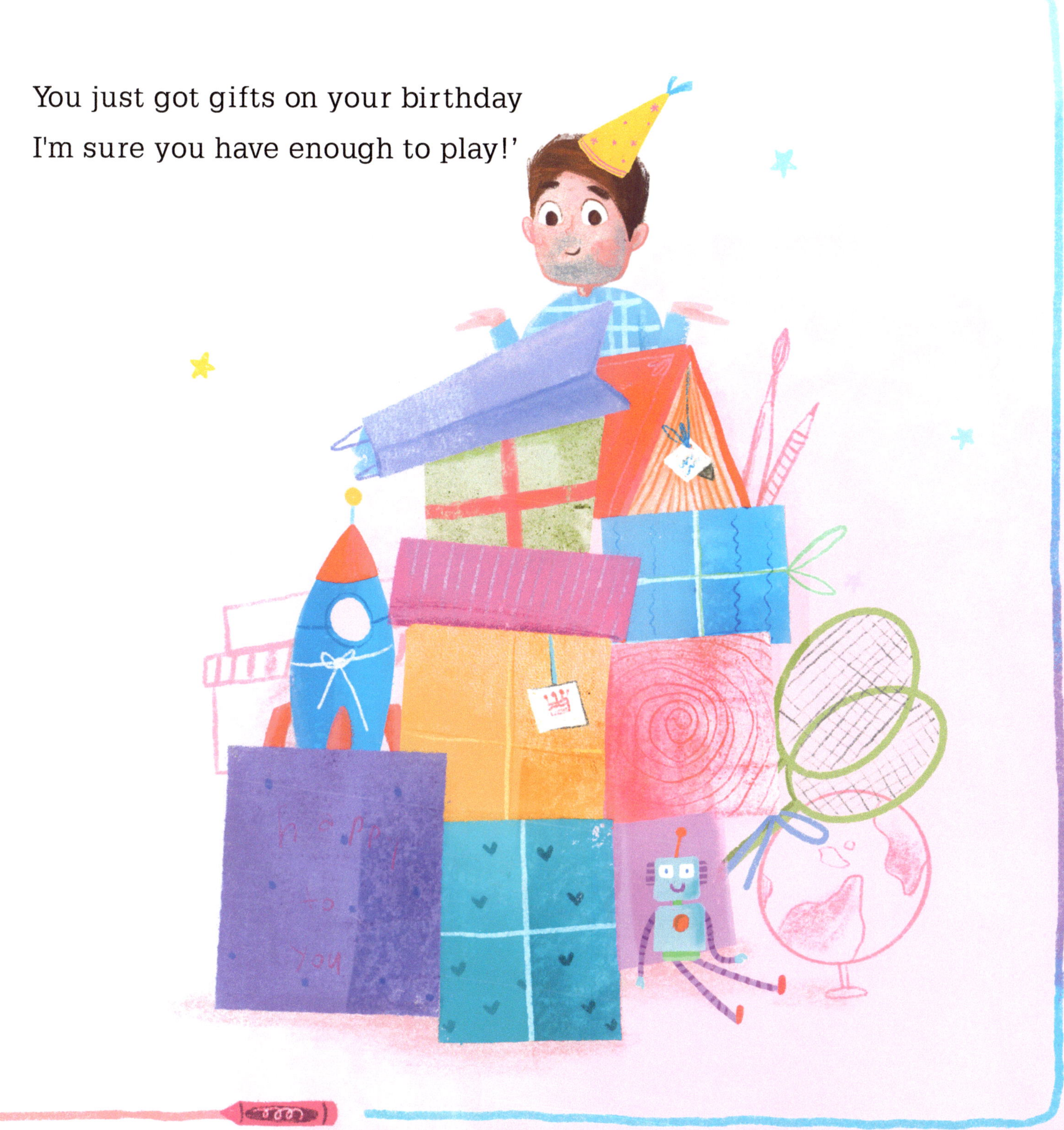

Lala dropped her shoulders

And crossed her arms in protest

'I just have a few nice toys

But I'm really bored of the rest'

‘Nina already has that dinosaur

And Tanya showed me her new game

My friends have lot more toys Papa

Why can't I also have the same?'

'I see how you feel' said Papa

‘But it's not nice to compare

You will always feel dissatisfied
And nothing will seem to be fair!'

‘We all get different gifts
Some get a few, some more

Each gift is precious you know
So why should we keep a score?'

‘When we keep asking for more

It makes us look greedy

If you have toys you don't want any more
Donate to kids who are needy'

'Be happy with you have

And fill your heart with gratitude

Everyone will be proud of you

If you develop this positive attitude'

‘I understand Papa, I really do’

Lala said nodding her head

'I promise not to compare again
And always remember what you just said'

'Let's go buy something for Nina

Before it is too late

Once I get back, I will find some toys
Which we can donate!'

What do you think?

- What gift do you want to buy for your friend's birthday?

- Can you think of a few things you are grateful for?

- Why is it not good to compare your gifts with your friends?

- Do you have anything you would like to donate?

- Have you read the Lala and Papa book Don't Be Afraid to Lose?

www.ingramcontent.com/pod-product-compliance
Lightning Source LLC
LaVergne TN
LVHW071231160826
845679LV00003B/960
9781068765308